D1335261

Help with
Homework

Mental
Maths

Here's a short note to parents:
It is recommended that an adult spends time
with a child while doing any kind of school practice,
to offer encouragement and guidance. Find a quiet place
to work, preferably at a table, and encourage your child to hold
his or her pen or pencil correctly. Try to work at your child's
pace and avoid spending too long on any one page or
activity. Most of all, emphasise the fun element of
what you are doing and enjoy this special
and exciting time!

Designed and illustrated by Jeannette O'Toole
Cover design by Dan Green
Educational consultant Nina Filipek

www.autumnchildrensbooks.co.uk

Pet problems

Find the stickers and put them in place.

Do these sums. Write the answers in the boxes.

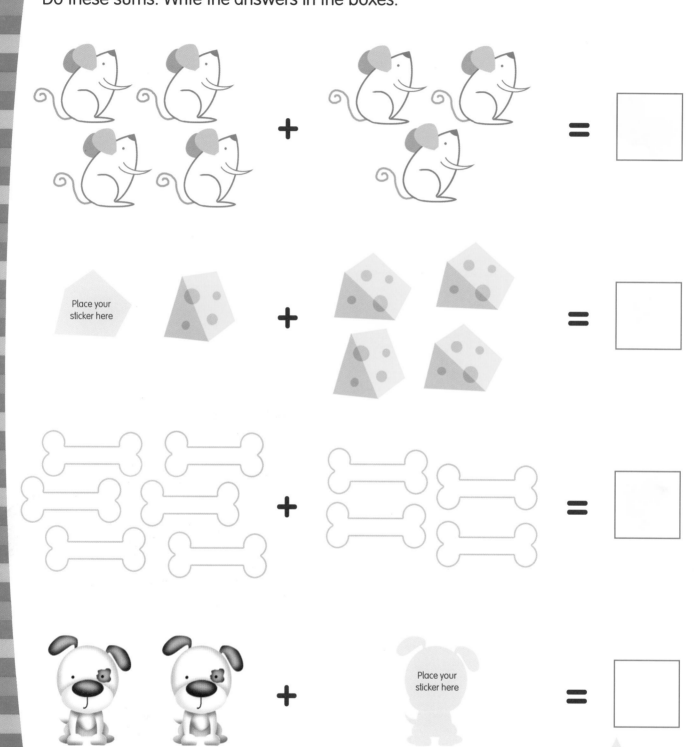

Adding numbers

As quickly as you can, add these numbers in your head and say the answers aloud.

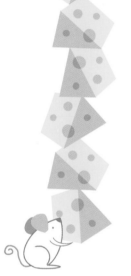

7 add 2	11 add 11
4 plus 4	9 plus 7
6 and 6	12 + 12
3 add 8	6 and 5
9 plus 4	eight plus two
7 + 7	9 add 8
5 and 5	11 plus 12
10 + 11	4 and 8
8 + 7	one add six
6 plus 8	5 + 10

Farmyard frolics

Answer the adding stories. Write the answers in the boxes and find the answer stickers.

There are **10** sheep. They meet up with **9** more sheep. How many sheep altogether?

Place your sticker here

Farmer Stan collects **3** hay bales on Monday, **2** on Tuesday and **3** on Wednesday. How many hay bales does he collect altogether?

Place your sticker here

One chicken lays **7** eggs and the other chicken lays **4** eggs. How many eggs altogether?

Place your sticker here

One pig has **3** piglets, another pig has **4** piglets and another pig has **5** piglets. How many piglets altogether?

Place your star sticker here

Pyramid puzzlers

Complete these adding pyramids. The first one has been done for you.
Write the numbers in the pyramids and find the number stickers.

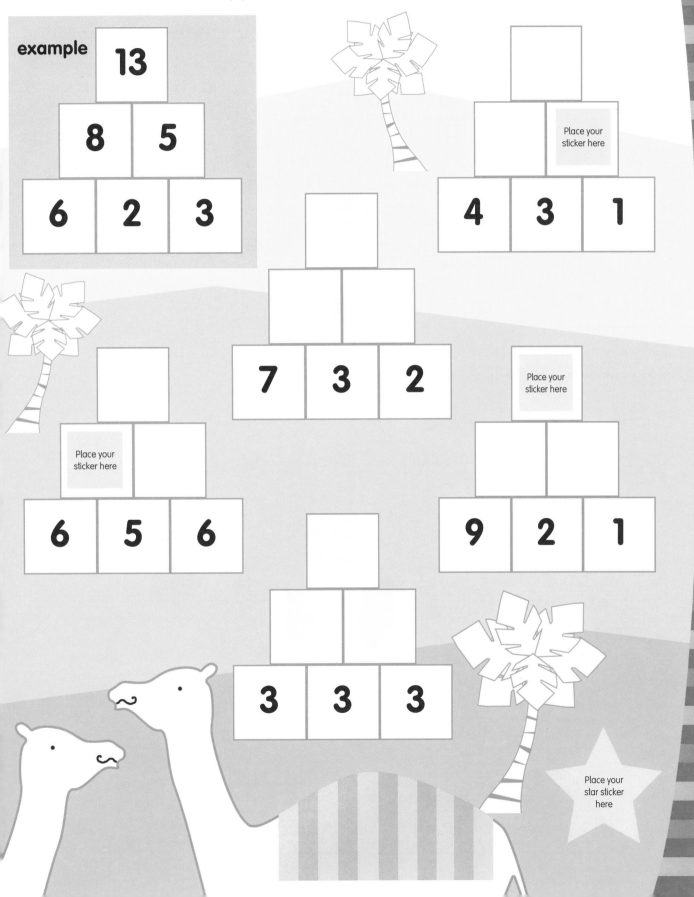

example

| 13 |
| 8 | 5 |
| 6 | 2 | 3 |

| 4 | 3 | 1 |

| 7 | 3 | 2 |

| 6 | 5 | 6 |

| 9 | 2 | 1 |

| 3 | 3 | 3 |

Place your sticker here

Place your sticker here

Place your sticker here

Place your star sticker here

Brain teasers

As quickly as you can, try answering these problems in your head.
Write the answers in the boxes and find the answer stickers.

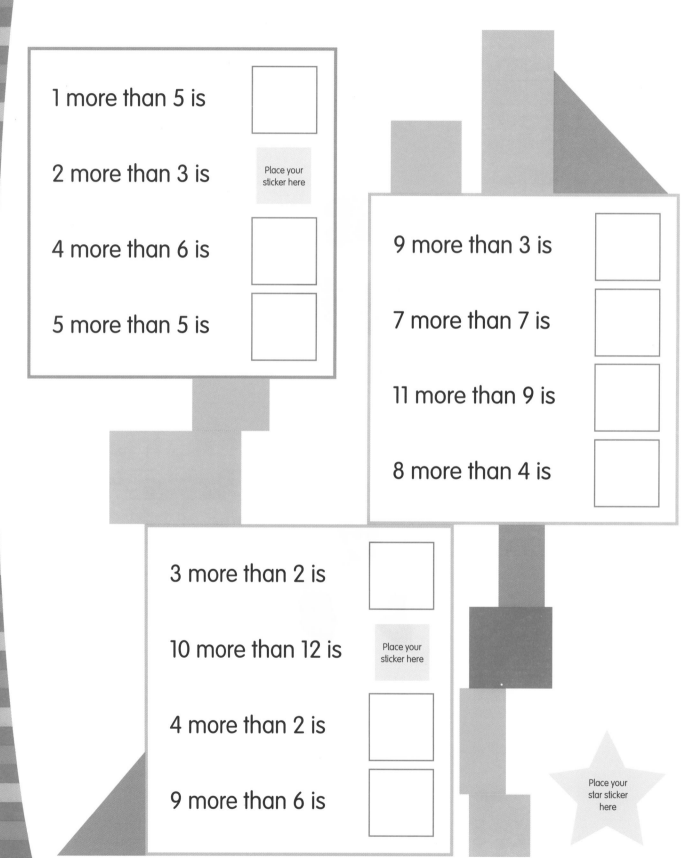

1 more than 5 is

2 more than 3 is

Place your sticker here

4 more than 6 is

5 more than 5 is

9 more than 3 is

7 more than 7 is

11 more than 9 is

8 more than 4 is

3 more than 2 is

10 more than 12 is

Place your sticker here

4 more than 2 is

9 more than 6 is

Place your star sticker here

Making 20

Draw horizontal or vertical lines to join two numbers next to each other that total **20**. You can use any of the numbers more than once.

7	2	19	1	4	7	14	3	17	5
11	19	20	4	16	15	7	2	15	1
9	15	5	1	2	8	5	15	3	0
5	3	12	2	2	6	20	19	17	19
10	13	2	18	0	12	20	0	6	20
10	20	5	9	4	5	0	1	14	6
15	10	2	16	16	4	3	6	6	7
11	4	13	7	1	6	1	19	7	1
3	9	8	2	4	0	19	7	8	8
6	11	9	0	2	20	2	3	0	12
1	1	7	5	3	1	2	6	11	9

Fishing for 20

Find the stickers and put them in place. As quickly as you can, draw lines to join the numbers on the penguins and fish that together total **20**. The first one has been done for you.

example

Seaside subtraction

Find the stickers and put them in place. Work out the sums, write the answers in the boxes and find the answer stickers.

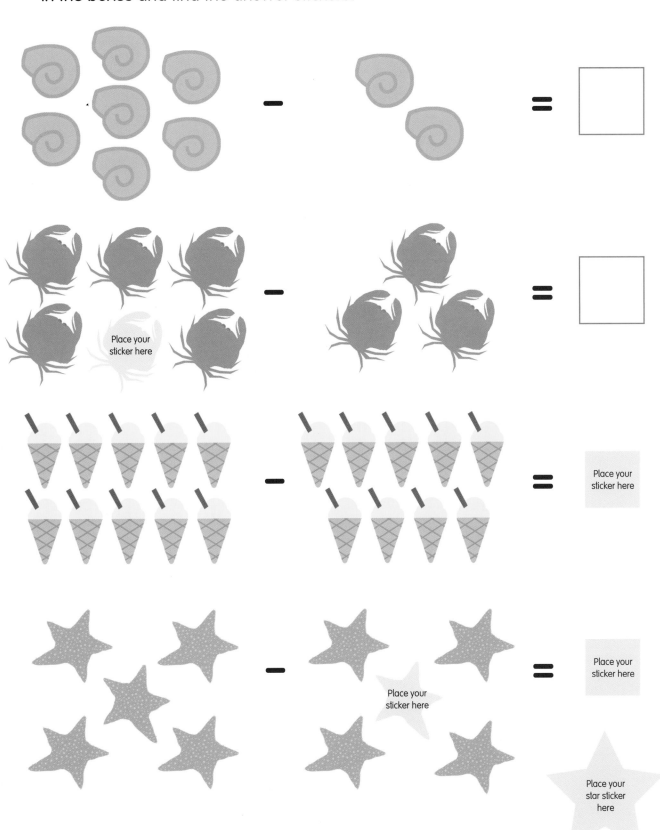

Subtracting numbers

Subtract these numbers in your head. Write the answers in the boxes and find the answer stickers.

12 minus 5 =

11 take away 7 equals | Place your sticker here

15 minus 5 =

10 take away 2 is

6 from 9 is

7 take away 4 is

3 subtract 2 equals

5 from 20 is

14 – 7 =

12 – 5 =

19 from 20 =

nine minus three equals | Place your sticker here

20 minus 17 equals

4 subtract 2 is

Place your star sticker here

Pond problems

Find the stickers and put them in place. Answer these subtracting stories.
Write the answers in the boxes and find the answer stickers.

There are **12** ducks on the pond, then **6** ducks fly away.

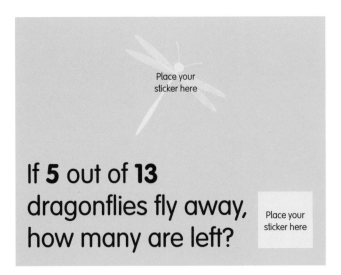

How many are left? ☐

Place your sticker here

14 frogs sit on the lily pads. If **8** frogs hop away, how many remain?

Place your sticker here

There are **18** snails by the pond. **6** snails slide away and **4** more follow them.

How many snails remain? ☐

Place your sticker here

If **5** out of **13** dragonflies fly away, how many are left?

Place your sticker here

Place your star sticker here

Baby blocks

Complete these subtracting blocks. The first one has been done for you.

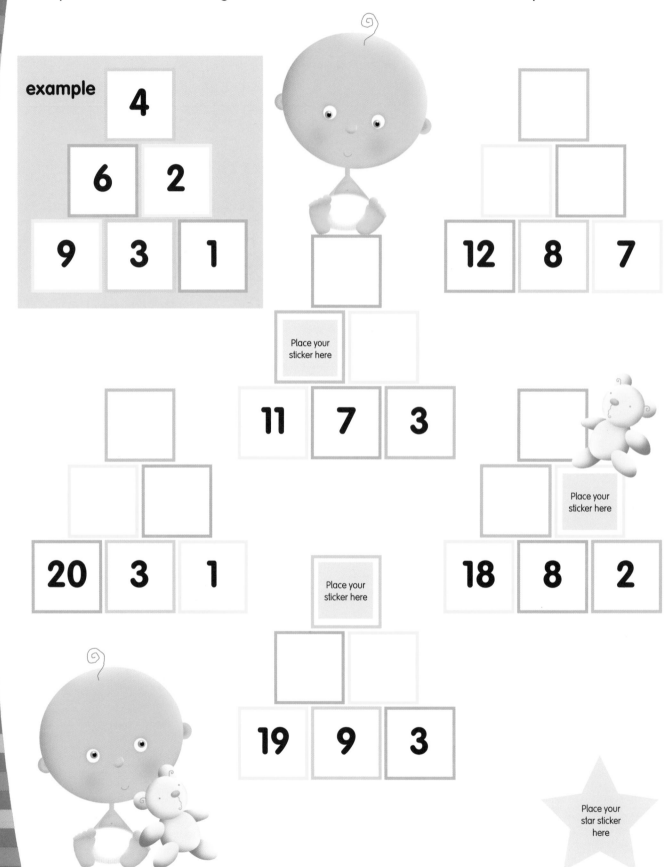

example

4

6 2

9 3 1

12 8 7

Place your sticker here

11 7 3

Place your sticker here

20 3 1

18 8 2

Place your sticker here

19 9 3

Place your star sticker here

Computer crazy

Colin the computer is feeling tired. Help him finish this table of calculations.
Write the numbers in the table and find the number stickers.
The first one has been done for you.

START	ADD	EQUALS	SUBTRACT	TOTAL
3	2	5	1	4
2	1	_	2	_
6	Place your sticker here	8	4	_
5	5	_	5	Place your sticker here
1	_	11	_	6
4	6	_	6	_

Place your
star sticker
here

Number patterns

Complete these number patterns. Write the missing numbers and find the number stickers.

| 1 | | 3 | | 5 | | 7 |

| | 9 | | 7 | | 5 | |

| 2 | | 6 | | 10 | | 14 |

| | 6 | | 12 | Place your sticker here | 18 | |

| 4 | | 12 | | 20 | | 28 |

| | 10 | | 20 | | 30 | |

| 100 | Place your sticker here | 98 | | 96 | | 94 |

Place your star sticker here

Number trails

Do these sums. Write the answers in the boxes and find the answer stickers.

2 + 3 + 5 = ☐

2 + 2 + 2 = ☐

6 + 1 + 3 = ☐

4 + 1 + 6 = ☐

7 + 2 + 3 = Place your sticker here

0 + 5 + 0 = ☐

4 + 3 + 4 = ☐

1 + 10 + 10 = Place your sticker here

9 + 3 + 3 = ☐

10 + 10 + 10 = ☐

Place your star sticker here

Number order

Find the stickers and put them in place. Write these sets of numbers in order. Start with the **lowest** number each time.

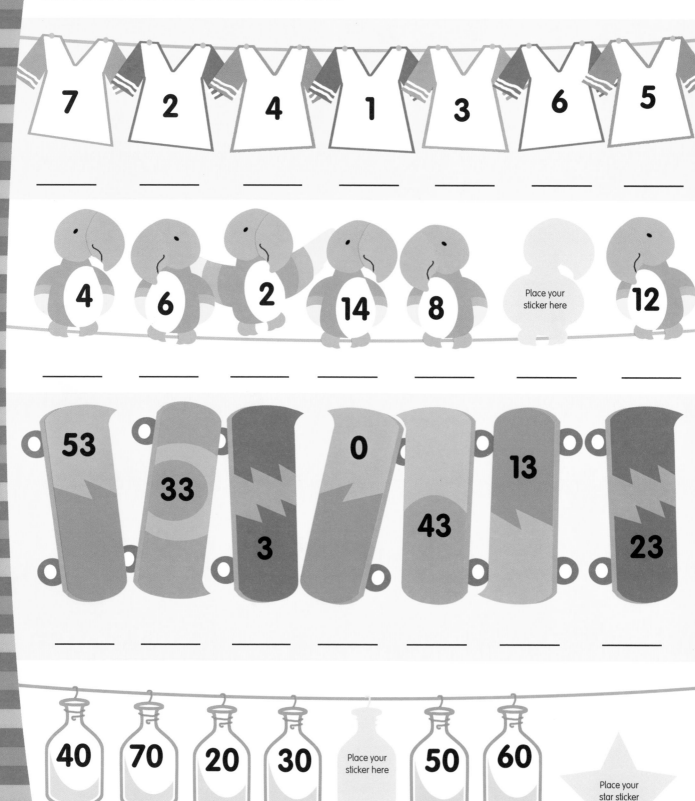

7   2   4   1   3   6   5

___   ___   ___   ___   ___   ___   ___

4   6   2   14   8   Place your sticker here   12

___   ___   ___   ___   ___   ___   ___

53   33   3   0   43   13   23

___   ___   ___   ___   ___   ___   ___

40   70   20   30   Place your sticker here   50   60

Place your star sticker here

___   ___   ___   ___   ___   ___   ___

8 11 4 11 14 5 22 1 0 4 6 6

8 4 6 4 2 5 15 99 12 21 11 3

50 1000   **144 100**

8 1 5 6 2 35 24 27 21

Up, up and away

Find the stickers and put them in place.

Draw lines to join pairs of numbers that total **20**.

Flying high

Find the missing kite stickers and put them in place.

Draw lines to join pairs of numbers that have a difference of **4**.

12

1

48

8

Place your
sticker here

30

44

Place your
sticker here

10

24

6

20

Place your
star sticker
here

Multiplication madness

The scientist has forgotten his times tables. Help him by completing these sums.

5 TIMES TABLES

1 X 5 =

2 X 5 =

3 X 5 =

4 X 5 =

5 X 5 =

6 X 5 =

7 X 5 =

9 TIMES TABLES

1 X 9 =

2 X 9 =

3 X 9 =

4 X 9 =

5 X 9 =

6 X 9 =

7 X 9 =

10 TIMES TABLES

1 X 10 =

2 X 10 =

3 X 10 =

4 X 10 =

5 X 10 =

6 X 10 =

7 X 10 =

7 TIMES TABLES

1 X 7 =

2 X 7 =

3 X 7 =

4 X 7 =

5 X 7 =

6 X 7 =

7 X 7 =

8 TIMES TABLES

1 X 8 =

2 X 8 =

3 X 8 =

4 X 8 =

5 X 8 =

6 X 8 =

7 X 8 =

Place your
star sticker
here

Skateboard sums

Find the stickers and put them in place. Draw lines to join the sums with their answers.

27

Place your
sticker here

60

5

6

21

33

65 – 5

8 x 8

7 x 3

60 ÷ 10

Place your
sticker here

3 x 9

10 ÷ 2

Place your
star sticker
here

Multiplying by 10

By adding **0** to the end of a number, you multiply it by **10**. Do these multiplications.
Write the answers in the boxes and find the answer stickers.

6 x 10 =

7 x 10 =

10 x 10 =

100 x 10 = Place your sticker here

1,000 x 10 =

1 x 10 =

2 x 10 =

3 x 10 =

4 x 10 =

5 x 10 = Place your sticker here

Place your star sticker here

Count with Dracula

Work out the sums in your head as quickly as you can.

3 × 2
4 × 9
20 ÷ 5
12 − 6
5 + 4
3 × 3
7 − 2

Place your sticker here

3 + 7
19 − 7
1 × 8
11 − 6
6 ÷ 2
7 − 3
8 + 2

8 × 3
5 − 5
15 ÷ 3
6 × 2
13 − 10
9 + 3
6 − 5

1 × 0
3 × 6
10 ÷ 1
5 × 4
18 − 5
9 + 2
1 + 1

Place your sticker here

Place your star sticker here

Dividing

Draw lines to join the divisions to their answers. Find the missing answer sticker.

$6 \div 2 =$

$10 \div 2 =$

$14 \div 2 =$

$60 \div 6 =$

$88 \div 8 =$

$5 \div 1 =$

$12 \div 3 =$

$12 \div 12 =$

$20 \div 10 =$

$6 \div 3 =$

$24 \div 6 =$

$14 \div 7 =$

3

4

5

1

2

10

7

2

Place your
sticker here

4

5

2

Place your
star sticker
here

Dividing by 10

By removing 0 from the end of a number, you divide it by 10. Do these divisions. Write the answers in the boxes and find the answer stickers.

10 ÷ 10 = ☐

20 ÷ 10 = ☐

30 ÷ 10 = Place your sticker here

40 ÷ 10 = ☐

50 ÷ 10 = ☐

60 ÷ 10 = ☐

70 ÷ 10 = ☐

80 ÷ 10 = Place your sticker here

90 ÷ 10 = ☐

100 ÷ 10 = ☐

Place your star sticker here

Double trouble

Find the sticker and put it in place. Double the numbers for these monster twins.

30

15

9

44

100

12

Place your sticker here

25

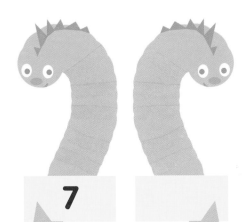

7

Place your star sticker here

Half the bother

Halve the numbers on each of the sails. Find the missing number stickers.

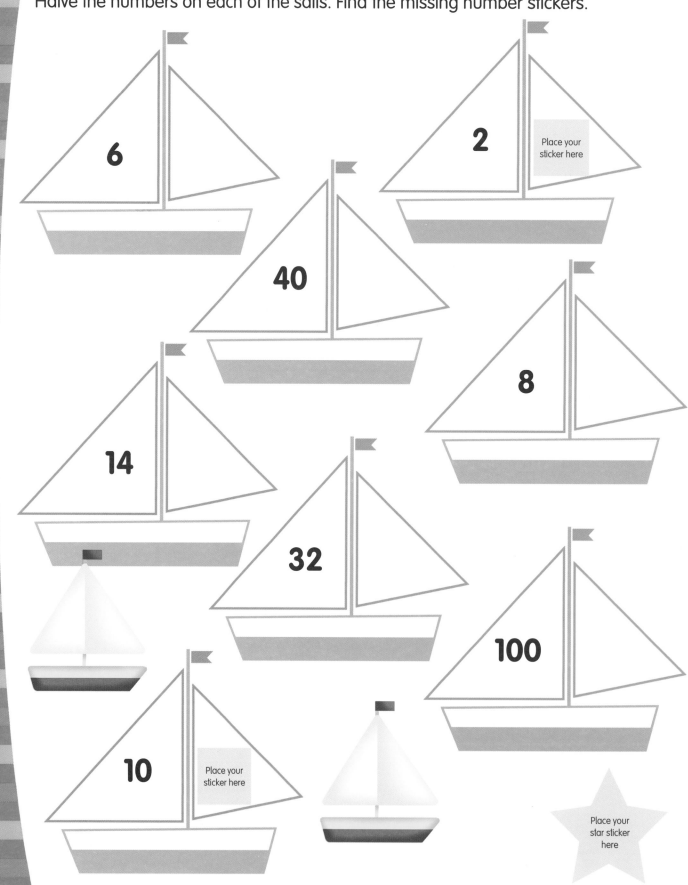

6

2

Place your
sticker here

40

8

14

32

100

10

Place your
sticker here

Place your
star sticker
here

Shapes

Write the answers in the boxes and find the answer stickers.

How many sides does a square have?

☐ sides

How many sides do 4 squares have altogether?

☐ sides

How many surfaces does a cube have?

Place your sticker here surfaces

How many sides does a triangle have?

☐ sides

How many sides do 7 triangles have altogether?

☐ sides

How many flat surfaces does a cylinder have?

Place your sticker here surfaces

Place your star sticker here

Speed test 1

Answer the questions as quickly as you can.
Write the answers in the boxes and find the answer stickers.

a) 7 add 13 is

b) What is 6 more than 12?

c) How many sides do 4 squares have altogether?

d) 12 × 12 = Place your sticker here

e) 5 eggs add 5 eggs take away 3 eggs equals

f) 10 × 10 = Place your sticker here

g) 9 buns divided between 3 elephants =

h) 2 + 14 + 6 =

i) subtract 7 from 30

j) 3 + 5 + 6 + 2 =

Place your star sticker here

Answer the questions as quickly as you can.
Write the answers in the boxes and find the answer stickers.

a) $100 \div 10 =$

b) $2 \times 2 \times 2 =$

c) add 20 to 15   Place your sticker here

d) There are 18 mice. The cat chases 6 mice.
How many are left?

e) 17 is how many more than 10?

f) $3 + 5 + 15 =$

g) 12 take away 7 equals

h) 19 add 5 is   Place your sticker here

i) 3 triangles have 6 sides altogether.
True or false?

j) $13 + 4 + 4 =$

Place your star sticker here

Speed test 3

Answer the questions as quickly as you can.
Write the answers in the boxes and find the answer stickers.

a) 7 birds from 13 birds equals

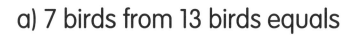

b) 4 ☐ 12 ☐ 20 ☐ 28 ☐ 36

c) A rectangle has 6 sides. True or false?

d) 3 x 3 x 3 = *Place your sticker here*

e) take 16 from 20

f) 10 x 9 =

g) If there are 14 fish in a net and 5 jump out, how many are left?

h) 8 + 13 = *Place your sticker here*

i) 4 + 7 + 2 + 1 + 0 =

j) ☐ 90 ☐ 70 ☐ 50 ☐ 30 ☐ 10

Place your star sticker here

Answers

Pet problems
4 + 3 = 7   2 + 4 = 6
6 + 4 = 10   2 + 1 = 3

Adding numbers
7 add 2 = 9   11 add 11 = 22
4 plus 4 = 8   9 plus 7 = 16
6 and 6 = 12   12 + 12 = 24
3 add 8 = 11   6 and 5 = 11
9 plus 4 = 13 eight plus two = 10
7 + 7 = 14   9 add 8 = 17
5 and 5 = 10   11 plus 12 = 23
10 + 11 = 21   4 and 8 = 12
8 + 7 = 15   one add six = 7
6 plus 8 = 14 5 + 10 = 15

Farmyard frolics
There are 19 sheep altogether.
Farmer Stan collects 8 hay bales altogether.
There are 11 eggs altogether.
There are 12 piglets altogether.

Pyramid puzzlers

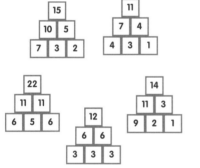

Brain teasers
1 more than 5 is 6
2 more than 3 is 5
4 more than 6 is 10
5 more than 5 is 10
9 more than 3 is 12
7 more than 7 is 14
11 more than 9 is 20
8 more than 4 is 12
3 more than 2 is 5
10 more than 12 is 22
4 more than 2 is 6
9 more than 6 is 15

Making 20

7	2	19	1	4	7	14	3	17	5
11	19	20	4	16	15	7	2	15	1
9	15	5	1	2	8	5	15	3	0
5	3	12	2	2	6	20	19	17	19
10	13	2	18	0	12	20	0	6	20
10	20	5	9	4	5	0	1	14	6
15	10	2	16	16	4	3	6	6	7
11	4	13	7	1	6	1	19	7	1
3	9	8	2	4	0	19	7	8	8
6	11	9	0	2	20	2	3	0	12
1	1	7	5	3	1	2	6	11	9

Fishing for 20
15 + 5 = 20   7 + 13 = 20
18 + 2 = 20   12 + 8 = 20
4 + 16 = 20   11 + 9 = 20
1 + 19 = 20   10 + 10 = 20

Seaside subtraction
7 – 2 = 5
6 – 3 = 3
10 – 9 = 1
5 – 5 = 0

Subtracting numbers
12 minus 5 = 7
11 take away 7 equals 4
15 minus 5 = 10
6 from 9 is 3
3 subtract 2 equals 1
14 – 7 = 7
19 from 20 = 1
10 take away 2 is 8
7 take away 4 is 3
5 from 20 is 15
12 – 5 = 7
nine minus three equals 6
20 minus 17 equals 3
4 subtract 2 is 2

Pond problems
6 ducks are left
6 frogs remain
8 dragonflies are left
8 snails remain

Baby blocks

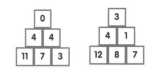
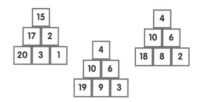

Computer crazy

START	ADD	EQUALS	SUBTRACT	TOTAL
3	2	5	1	4
2	1	3	2	1
6	2	8	4	4
5	5	10	5	5
1	10	11	5	6
4	6	10	6	4

Number patterns
1 2 3 4 5 6 7
10 9 8 7 6 5 4
2 4 6 8 10 12 14
3 6 9 12 15 18 21
4 8 12 16 20 24 28
5 10 15 20 25 30 35
100 99 98 97 96 95 94

Number trails
2 + 3 + 5 = 10
2 + 2 + 2 = 6
6 + 1 + 3 = 10
4 + 1 + 6 = 11
7 + 2 + 3 = 12
0 + 5 + 0 = 5
4 + 3 + 4 = 11
1 + 10 + 10 = 21
9 + 3 + 3 = 15
10 + 10 + 10 = 30

Number order
1 2 3 4 5 6 7
2 4 6 8 10 12 14
0 3 13 23 33 43 53
10 20 30 40 50 60 70

Answers

Up, up and away
0 + 20 = 20
1 + 19 = 20
7 + 13 = 20
10 + 10 = 20
17 + 3 = 20
12 + 8 = 20

Flying high
1 and 5   30 and 34
6 and 10   8 and 12
44 and 48   20 and 24

Multiplication madness
1 x 5 = 5   1 x 9 = 9
2 x 5 = 10   2 x 9 = 18
3 x 5 = 15   3 x 9 = 27
4 x 5 = 20   4 x 9 = 36
5 x 5 = 25   5 x 9 = 45
6 x 5 = 30   6 x 9 = 54
7 x 5 = 35   7 x 9 = 63

1 x 10 = 10   1 x 7 = 7
2 x 10 = 20   2 x 7 = 14
3 x 10 = 30   3 x 7 = 21
4 x 10 = 40   4 x 7 = 28
5 x 10 = 50   5 x 7 = 35
6 x 10 = 60   6 x 7 = 42
7 x 10 = 70   7 x 7 = 49

1 x 8 = 8
2 x 8 = 16
3 x 8 = 24
4 x 8 = 32
5 x 8 = 40
6 x 8 = 48
7 x 8 = 56

Skateboard sums
65 – 5 = 60
21 + 12 = 33
8 x 8 = 64
60 ÷ 10 = 6
3 x 9 = 27
7 x 3 = 21
10 ÷ 2 = 5

Multiplying by 10
1 x 10 = 10
2 x 10 = 20
3 x 10 = 30
4 x 10 = 40
5 x 10 = 50
6 x 10 = 60
7 x 10 = 70
10 x 10 = 100
100 x 10 = 1,000
1,000 x 10 = 10,000

Count with Dracula
3 x 2 = 6   8 x 3 = 24
4 x 9 = 36   5 – 5 = 0
20 ÷ 5 = 4   15 ÷ 3 = 5
12 – 6 = 6   6 x 2 = 12
5 + 4 = 9   13 – 10 = 3
3 x 3 = 9   9 + 3 = 12
7 – 2 = 5   6 – 5 = 1

3 + 7 = 10   1 x 0 = 0
19 – 7 = 12   3 x 6 = 18
1 x 8 = 8   10 ÷ 1 = 10
11 – 6 = 5   5 x 4 = 20
6 ÷ 2 = 3   18 – 5 = 13
7 – 3 = 4   9 + 2 = 11
8 + 2 = 10   1 + 1 = 2

Dividing
6 ÷ 2 = 3   12 ÷ 3 = 4
10 ÷ 2 = 5   12 ÷ 12 = 1
14 ÷ 2 = 7   20 ÷ 10 = 2
60 ÷ 6 = 10   6 ÷ 3 = 2
88 ÷ 8 = 11   24 ÷ 6 = 4
5 ÷ 1 = 5   14 ÷ 7 = 2

Dividing by 10
10 ÷ 10 = 1
20 ÷ 10 = 2
30 ÷ 10 = 3
40 ÷ 10 = 4
50 ÷ 10 = 5
60 ÷ 10 = 6
70 ÷ 10 = 7
80 ÷ 10 = 8
90 ÷ 10 = 9
100 ÷ 10 = 10

Double trouble
30 – 60   15 – 30
44 – 88   9 – 18
12 – 24   100 – 200
7 – 14   25 – 50

Half the bother
6 – 3   2 – 1
40 – 20   8 – 4
14 – 7   32 – 16
10 – 5   100 – 50

Shapes
A square has 4 sides.
4 squares have 16 sides.
A cube has 6 surfaces.
A triangle has 3 sides.
7 triangles have 21 sides.
A cylinder has 2 flat surfaces.

Speed test 1
a) 20   b) 18
c) 16   d) 144
e) 7   f) 100
g) 3   h) 22
i) 23   j) 16

Speed test 2
a) 10   b) 8
c) 35   d) 12
e) 7   f) 23
g) 5   h) 24
i) false   j) 21

Speed test 3
a) 6 birds
b) 8 16 24 32
c) false
d) 27
e) 4
f) 90
g) 9
h) 21
i) 14
j) 100 80 60 40 20